ALL ABOUT AMBER:
PLANNING FOR OUR DOG
IN THE EVENT OF OUR PASSING

By: Charlene Densen and
Robert Schonfeld

First published by Dog Ear Publishing
4010 W. 86th Street, Ste H
Indianapolis, IN 46268
www.dogearpublishing.net

ISBN: 978-160844-480-9

This book is printed on acid-free paper.

Printed in the United States of America

Dear Grandma and Uncle Craig:

Amber is seven years old. The life expectancy of a Pomeranian is approximately 15 years. Therefore, if the life expectancy tables are correct with regard to Amber and us, we will survive Amber.

However, as you know, strange things can happen in life. No one expected cousin Alan to die of a heart attack on his fiftieth birthday. Both of us lost acquaintances younger than us on 9/11.

Both of our wills would give Amber to you upon our passing. If Amber survives us, we would want Amber to be cared for in the manner and style in which she is accustomed. That means your getting to know and understand Amber, even though you live more than one thousand miles away from us.

Therefore, we present you with this guide to Amber. It looks complicated, and Amber does require a high degree of maintenance. However, she is the love of our lives and would be the love of your lives if she were to survive us. She will be worth every moment of your time, and you will want to spend every possible moment with her.

In the Beginning

Amber was born on October 13, 2002 to a breeder in Missouri. We have her family tree, which includes a Champion and dogs of several different colors including cream, black and her primary color, red-orange.

We wrote to Amber's breeder asking for pictures of her parents. Unfortunately, we did not receive an answer back. We have little idea what Amber's first nine weeks were like, and always wonder how Amber would react if she were taken back to visit her first home.

Before leaving Missouri, Amber was microchipped with the American Kennel Club and given appropriate vaccinations. In the event she gets lost, details about Amber can be located in a registry with the American Kennel Club—you have to update the data when appropriate. Veterinarians and shelters have a machine that can read the microchip in the back of her neck. Amber's microchip information and all of her medical records are contained in a looseleaf package which we have prepared for you.

In mid-December, 2002, Amber was separated from her mother at nine weeks old and placed on a truck to New York. The trip was 20 hours—can you imagine being separated from your mother at nine weeks old and placed in a cage on a truck in mid-December for a 20-hour trip halfway across the country to a strange place?

A week before Christmas, Mommy called a nearby pet store to see if it had any Pomeranians. Mommy and Daddy had wanted a Pomeranian for years but could not find the right one. However, on that day, the pet store Mommy had called said that a female Pomeranian had just been unloaded from a truck. The pet store, which was operated by a man who hosted a show on pets on a local television station and appeared on Martha Stewart's show as a pet expert, had an excellent reputation.

Mommy immediately went to meet the Pomeranian. The Pomeranian was at first nervous—who wouldn't be after being separated from their mother at nine weeks old and placed on a truck for a 20-hour trip across the country? However, Mommy played with the Pomeranian and the Pomeranian warmed up to Mommy and displayed considerable personality. Mommy was sure that this was the right one. Mommy brought Daddy back that evening to play with the Pomeranian, and Daddy agreed. Mommy and Daddy shopped around to look at other Pomeranians that weekend, but both of us fell in love with this Pomeranian. This Pomeranian was special—she had spirit and personality and as you say, Grandma, a little bit of devil in her. We placed a deposit on her, and the store said that it wanted to keep her a few more days so that she would gain some more weight.

Unfortunately, we had to go to a funeral the next day, and we started to have second thoughts about what it would be like to adopt a dog. Both of us worked five-day weeks at that time, and we had just purchased an apartment in a condominium that did not allow dogs. Daddy returned to the store to remove the deposit. However, when he went back to the store, the Pomeranian was there and gave Daddy a dirty look, as to say: "don't you dare remove that deposit, I'm coming home with you."

The next day, which was Christmas Eve, Daddy could not work. He kept thinking about the Pomeranian and how she needed a home for Christmas. Daddy called Mommy, and late Christmas Eve afternoon, we adopted the Pomeranian. She was less than three pounds, had a black, raccoon-looking face, and was practically all fur. We bought some baby gates to block off the steps to the lower level of our apartment, some wee-wee pads, some dog food, and at the suggestion of the pet store, a cage for training.

We brought her back to our apartment that evening. The first person Amber met in our apartment building was a member of the New York Jets and Amber has since seen and met quite a few celebrities, including Donald Trump, Rudolph Giuliani, baseball players Frank Robinson and Pedro Martinez, writers Carl Bernstein and Judith Miller, and Dylan Lauren, the daughter of Ralph Lauren and the owner of Dylan's candy stores.

Amber ate her dog food, urinated on her wee-wee pad and scampered around the apartment. Late that evening, we placed Amber in the cage. Amber started to bang her head against the cage and scream. Apparently, Amber had had a bad experience with cages, either at her breeder or on the truck. We thought Amber was going to have a heart attack or a concussion, and we called you, Grandma, for advice. Taking your advice, we removed Amber from the cage and let her spend the night with us. We never placed Amber in a cage again, and gave the cage to a charity. Years later, if we bring Amber anywhere where there are cages, she gets very nervous and shakes and we have to take her away immediately. You can never put Amber in a cage—otherwise, we will come back to haunt you.

We selected Amber's name from a list of dog names on a website. At the time we chose the name, Amber was more sable color than amber color. As Amber is now amber color, she literally grew into her name. Her nicknames are "Bam," "Angel Face" and "Beauty Queen."

Amber toilet-trained fairly easy and her first veterinary visits were uneventful. After chewing on the furniture during the first month, Amber settled down and has turned out to be as well-behaved a dog as one can imagine.

As it was a cold, snowy winter, Amber's first few months were spent largely at home. When Mommy and Daddy were at work during the weekdays, Amber spent her days in the kitchen behind a baby gate. Daddy would come home for lunch to make sure she was well. Eventually, Amber learned how to open the kitchen gate by herself and had the run of the upstairs of the apartment. Her appearance began to change—the black, raccoon-like markings faded and her ears which were curved became pointy.

In March, we brought Amber to a puppy kindergarten class. She did not love the other dogs in the class. Amber never got the hang of walking through a tunnel or the other agility exercises. However, we noticed that when we walked Amber around the perimeter of the room where the kindergarten was held, Amber greeted the people as if she were a politician and the people around the room greeted her back. We realized then that there was something special about Amber, that she reacted extremely well to people and vice versa, and that she really preferred people to other dogs.

We did not choose to spay Amber as a puppy. Spaying involves anesthesia, and we were concerned about anesthetizing a dog as small as Amber. Daddy lost a friend at age 43 who went in for a minor operation at an excellent hospital and was overanesthetized.

We realized that there were risks in not spaying Amber. We were aware that Amber could develop pyometra, a life-threatening condition requiring the immediate removal of her uterus. We were also aware that Amber being unspayed was more susceptible to cancer than a spayed dog, not to mention the blood we had to clean up every seven months when she was in season. Nonetheless, we weighed the benefits and risks of spaying and decided to let Amber remain intact. We believed that by constantly monitoring her, we could see if there was anything unusual or wrong and take immediate steps to resolve any problem.

Unfortunately, as you know, Amber did develop pyometra. Fortunately, because of our constant monitoring, we caught it in the very early stages. Amber's operation was uneventful and her recovery was swift. She is now spayed and she will not have any further bloody heat cycles. However, we still have to monitor her for cancer. We especially check her nipples to make sure they do not change in size, shape or color.

Finally, Amber is much larger than the typical Pomeranian, and her long build is different from the squat stature of most Pomeranians. Therefore, please don't embarrass Amber by placing her in a dog show unless it is a contest for cutest dog or best dressed dog in a Halloween parade. Dog shows generally measure whether a dog conforms to breed standards, and Amber does not conform to breed standards. You could not imagine a better dog than Amber as a companion, but she does not conform to Pomeranian standards.

Amber as a baby with her first toys.

Early picture of Amber on pillows.

Amber near her baby gate.

Amber's first Valentine's Day outfit.

Basic Personality Traits

Amber is a dog that wants to be part of the family. As you know, dogs as a species are pack animals that do not want to be alone. Amber wants to go all of the places Mommy and Daddy go. She gets very upset when she is left at home without Mommy and Daddy and, if left alone, wildly greets Mommy and Daddy when they return. She also wants to eat all of the food Mommy and Daddy are eating, even if the food is not good for her.

When Amber was younger, she screamed when Daddy would go to work. She has since gotten used to that and realizes that Daddy goes to work to make sure that she can eat the best food and be dressed in the finest clothing. Still, she sometimes does not get the concept of "casual Friday." Amber understands that if Daddy wears a suit and tie, it means that he is going to work and she must stay home. Amber also understands that if Daddy dresses casually, he usually stays home with her. Amber sometimes does not understand why Daddy dresses casually on Friday and does not stay home with her.

Mommy and Daddy used to have "date night" every week, but we do that less frequently so that we can eat virtually all of our meals with Amber. We view Amber as being a "limited engagement"—like a child who has a rare disease and will only live into her teens. We will likely have plenty of time to travel and eat in fine restaurants after Amber is gone, so we would rather enjoy our time with Amber while she is here. Remember, one dog year equals seven human years, so that if Amber has a bad day, that is the equivalent to us having a bad week.

Amber travels everywhere with us. Since we have adopted Amber, we have not gone on a vacation without Amber and would never put her in a kennel where she would be caged.

Amber is curious about life and loves to explore. While on walks, she will sniff everything, and stop to watch and observe the slightest human activity, whether it is a family unloading bundles from a car or placing a child on a school bus. We take Amber on dog walks to raise money for charity. Instead of walking straight ahead like the other dogs, Amber will stop and sniff everything and is usually one of the last dogs to cross the finish line.

One of Amber's favorite activities is to sit in the lobby of our building and greet the other residents coming home at night or coming off of the elevator. The residents call her the "mayor" or the "queen" of the lobby. She also likes to sit on our oceanfront terrace to watch the surfers, the kites and the people walking the boardwalk.

Amber will want to share exploration and play time with you. When she is in the backyard of our summer home in the Hamptons and she sees a rabbit or squirrel in our neighbors' yard, she will bark at the animal and then come over to you, smile, and then ask you to join her in viewing the animal. She will want you to throw toys down the hall so she can retrieve them and ask you to throw them again. She is also into "sneak attacks," like stealing Mommy's schruncie from Mommy's hair.

Amber is very smart. As we will discuss later, she knows several words in English and what they refer to. She is always very aware of where she is. There is a dog store in the center of a small town on Eastern Long Island that we visit every few months. Wherever we park in that town, Amber drags Daddy straight to the dog store for a cookie. She has a fantastic memory for places she may have been once or twice and places she had not been for a while.

As you well know, Amber is beautiful. Because of her beauty and her love of people, people react well to her. Besides having won a "Dog of the Month" contest on a local television station, she is on a video on "You Tube" promoting a book by a prominent cartoonist. Pictures of her at a cocktail party and a dog walk for the Animal Rescue Fund of the Hamptons (a no-kill shelter) were published in the newspaper. She has been oil painted, caricatured, and turned into a ceramic figure.

Amber is the epitome of "cute." From her little prance around the house, to her curling up to Mommy in the back seat of the car to her little growl if she wants something, Amber is just plain cute.

Amber can be sensitive at times. She cannot tolerate some smells and got sick when our building caulked the exterior of the windows with toxic caulking materials. She does not like loud sudden noises like from motorcycles or street cleaners or sudden movements like signs or flags blowing in the wind. Amber especially does not like any displays of anger or, in general, outbursts of emotions. Like human beings, Amber has emotions and feelings and those emotions and feelings have to be respected.

Above all, Amber smiles almost all of the time and appears to be secure, content and happy. Please do everything you can to keep her that way.

Amber's signature prance.

Amber interviewed on Plum TV after winning
"Dog of the Month" contest.

Health

Your most important mission is to keep Amber healthy. There are many things you must know about Pomeranians in general and Amber in particular to keep her healthy.

There are two medical issues that affect most Pomeranians and both will affect Amber. One is breathing. Pomeranians have trachea problems, which was something we considered when we chose not to put Amber through anesthesia when she was a puppy. Amber can breathe heavy in warm and humid weather. Therefore, you will have to make sure that she always has fresh cool air and air conditioning. Amber loves air conditioning, and insists on it in the car at full blast even if it's 35 degrees outside and Mommy and Daddy are freezing.

If you must carry Amber, remember to carry her by placing your arm around her rear end rather than her midsection. The less pressure around where Amber breathes, the better.

The second issue is her legs. Amber's rear right (when you face her) leg has a luxating patella—the joint occasionally goes out of place when she walks. The leg is lazy and she sometimes leans on the leg when sitting. This is fairly common for Pomeranians.

Amber may also have arthritis in this leg. She may eventually need surgery for this—her veterinarian has said that her condition is a 3 on a scale of 4 which is not good—but it seems to have improved a bit in recent years.

If you see Amber limp in the back, pick her up and massage the leg. Make sure that Amber does not jump off furniture or beds or stay in her dog stroller too long—more about the stroller later. Also, please watch Amber's weight—the less weight she places on her rear legs, the better.

Amber has had an allergic reaction to doggy shampoo and we generally have her bathed in either Johnson's Baby Shampoo or oatmeal shampoo. She has also had a bad reaction to chemicals placed in the grass of our Hamptons summer home. Amber has chronic runny eyes which must constantly be cleaned. (She loves to eat the dirt from her eyes, of which Mommy disapproves.) Once in a while, Amber will develop sores on her back near the tail known as "hot spots." They are nothing to worry about, and if she has them, just bathe her in oatmeal shampoo. Also, Amber sometimes drinks water too quickly and appears to be choking. Be patient and assure her that everything is OK.

Prior to her operation for pyometra, her most serious condition came when she was three years old. Daddy noticed one morning while walking with her that she was squatting too frequently and that nothing was coming out. A few days later, he noticed that Amber was urinating blood. As you will learn, you must know Amber's habits well so that if you see something unusual, you can act quickly.

We immediately brought her to the veterinarian, who determined after a urinalysis and blood test that she had a urinary tract infection. The vet prescribed antibiotics. Unfortunately, the antibiotics did not help Amber who, in general, does not handle antibiotics and internal medication well.

We brought Amber to a more specialized hospital, which took a sonogram and determined that she had a stone that could eventually block her ability to urinate. The stone, we were told, had to come out immediately. We sought a second opinion from the Animal Medical Center in New York City, one of the leading veterinary hospitals in the country. That hospital agreed with the first hospital. We compared the facilities, the doctors, and especially, the anesthesia protocols of the two hospitals, and we opted for the Animal Medical Center to perform the surgery.

Amber's surgery was successful. Amber spent much of the time after her surgery at Daddy's office where she recovered nicely in the company of Daddy's secretaries Aunt Karen and Aunt Kelli. Amber helped Daddy in composing a will, in drafting a contract, and in a closing on a house. Amber and Daddy visited the McDonald's drive-up every day for lunch and dined on grilled chicken.

To ensure that no new stones would form, Daddy called a dog nutritionist in Boston to create a diet for Amber. The nutritionist recommended a diet of protein and carbs with a little bit of calcium and salt thrown in. The diet, which is in her looseleaf folder, works and Amber has been stone-free since the operation.

The game plan is to keep the ph level of Amber's urine low (more acidic) to impede the development of new stones. For her annual check-ups, we try to obtain urine from Amber in a urine cup (known as "free catch") as the other alternative would not be pleasant for Amber. However, Amber is not always that cooperative and the sight of Daddy trying to collect urine from Amber is pretty funny.

We have one special secret weapon. We learned that blueberries are acidic and good for keeping the ph levels low.

Unfortunately, Amber does not like pure blueberries. However, Amber loves blueberry muffins, and Daddy and Amber go to the Starbucks drive-up every morning for coffee (for Daddy), ice water (for Amber) and a blueberry muffin. Several generations of Starbucks employees have met and greeted Amber and know her by name.

Amber loves her present veterinarian. Since you are not in metropolitan New York and will have to choose a new veterinarian, choose a female veterinarian as she seems to prefer female veterinarians. Amber is up-to-date on all of her shots and we have a looseleaf book with the history of all of her medical visits.

Amber has an annual checkup and receives a rabies shot every three years and her other shots roughly every two years. At her annual checkups, have a titer test performed on her to determine whether she actually needs the shots. We do not want her to receive any more medication than necessary.

Amber receives a heartworm tablet once a month with her dinner in the spring, summer and fall and flea and tick medication in the summer. If you remain in Florida, you will have to give her these medications the entire year.

Please do whatever you can to stay with Amber while she is receiving any medical attention and bring a blanket to all vet visits as she does not like to sit on the cold metal examining tables. We are reluctant to give Amber to a veterinarian to perform any test not in our presence, and as you already know, Amber cannot be placed in a cage for any length of time. Ask a lot of questions of your veterinarian, and don't be shy about getting second opinions. If internal medication is prescribed, try to determine if it is really necessary as Amber does not do well with internal medication. And if what the veterinarian says does not make sense to you, it probably does not make sense.

If you have to give Amber any medication, try natural remedies. On a similar note, as Amber appears to be sensitive to chemicals and certain smells, try using natural or green products in cleaning the house and perfume-free or baby laundry detergent. We avoid air fresheners and chemicals for extermination and unclogging drains and we even shine our shoes with shoe polish on the outdoor terrace rather than in the apartment.

Make sure that you know the phone number and location of a 24/7 emergency vet or animal hospital. We have never needed one for Amber, and hopefully we never will.

We have a dog veterinary book at home to explain medical matters if Amber acts out of the ordinary. The Internet is also a great source of veterinary information on dogs. The most important thing is to watch to see if Amber is doing anything unusual—diarrhea, loss of appetite, biting or licking parts of her body, etc.

Hygiene

Amber would not fare well with a traditional groomer. With a regular groomer, you would have to drop Amber off, Amber would be caged, and you would pick her up several hours later. Obviously, that would not work for Amber.

Instead, Amber's puppy kindergarten teacher grooms her once a month in her home. That includes some trimming of her fur, a bath, a blow dry, and the grinding of her nails. Mommy and Daddy stay with her for the half-hour of grooming and the groomer is always a source of valuable information on dogs in general and dog events in our area. You will need to find someone like our puppy kindergarten teacher in your area to groom Amber.

Amber was not always thrilled with grooming. Initially, the groomer clipped Amber's nails and that was always a struggle for all. Amber's nails were clipped too short by her first veterinarian— she was in pain from the clipping and remembered the pain. Fortunately, the groomer bought a grinder for her own whippet and it worked for Amber as well.

If Amber rolls around in goose dung as she loves to do or has had a particularly messy doody, we try to bathe her immediately. The water must be lukewarm, not too hot and not too cold. Amber will tolerate us blow drying her, but only for a few minutes. Although Amber can get dirty, we don't wish to prevent her from doing anything she enjoys doing, as long as it is not harmful to her.

In Florida, you may be tempted to cut Amber's thick coat off in the summer in what is sometimes called a "lion cut". Don't do it. Amber needs the coat to protect her from the sun, insects, skin cancer, and the heat, and we have heard horror stories about Pomeranians that received lion cuts.

We brush Amber's hair as often as possible. Amber likes that, especially if you kiss her while brushing her. Watch out for her rear, though, as Amber does not particularly like her rear touched by anyone but Mommy. You will notice that there is a portion of the tip of the tail that doesn't have hair— don't worry about that.

Amber's teeth should be brushed once a week. She does not like the traditional doggy toothbrushes and prefers little brushes you can place on your finger (we call them "finger puppets"). Amber likes peanut butter or chicken flavor doggy toothpaste.

Finally, you will be glad to know that Amber does shed her coat once or twice a year. Use a brush to take the hair out.

Food

Amber loves food, as long as it does not come from a package that has a picture of a dog.

As we mentioned before, Amber's diet requires her to have a mixture of protein and carbs. Amber's favorite protein is chicken. She has eaten chicken from Italian, Chinese, Japanese, Thai, Indian, French, German, Greek, Spanish, Portuguese, Mexican, Russian and Kosher restaurants. She likes grilled chicken (easy on the spices and herbs), steamed chicken, roasted chicken, and barbeque chicken. We try to avoid fried or breaded chicken, even though Amber likes breading on her chicken. Amber likes her chicken moist and prefers dark meat.

Amber also likes steak and hamburgers (medium well), lamb chops (also medium well), turkey, brisket, roast beef, bison burgers, liver, turkey burgers and turkey steaks. She likes eggs but not egg whites. She does not like fish or leftovers, and doesn't particularly like smoked or highly seasoned meats.

As for carbs, Amber loves pasta, especially when moist. Thick pastas like rigatoni or penne are easier to feed her then spaghetti or linguini. She loves carrots, rice, squash, corn, peas, sweet potatoes, yams, and zucchini. She also loves apples and cantaloupe. Her guilty pleasures are French fries, lettuce, bread, bagels, pizza crust, and licking out clam shells, none of which is wonderful for dogs.

While Amber does not love dog food, we do mix some into her people food from time to time. Amber prefers dog food that looks like stew (such as Spot's Stew) to dog food that looks like paté.

We try to mix Amber's meat and carbs together, but sometimes she likes to pick out what she wants. For example, if we serve her meat and potatoes, she may pick out the meat from the potatoes. Don't let her do that. We try to give her two vegetables in the event she doesn't like one of them, and we often mix in small amounts of lettuce and bread to get her started as she sometimes turns her nose up at her meal. She also has to see where the food is coming from (the original plate from which it is served) and often prefers to eat from Mommy or Daddy's meal even if it is the same meal as hers. If she smells food that she likes better than her own meal (such as fries, lettuce or bread), she will stop eating her meal until she receives some of the food she really wants.

There will also be days where Amber may be hesitant to eat and you may have to hand feed her. Also, if Amber has to make a doody, she may decline to eat until she is given the opportunity to walk and defecate.

Amber is not a pig—she tells you when she has eaten enough and rarely throws up. If Amber signals that she wants water, the end of the meal is near.

No-nos for Amber include chocolate, onions, raisins, grapes, tomatoes, broccoli, string beans, cheese, shellfish (except for clamshells), pork products, dairy products (except for doggy ice cream, which she loves), avocado, nuts and citrus products. Amber should not have heavy sauces and spices, but she does like her food dipped in something. Olive oil works fine, and it is good for her.

As Amber is part of the family, she eats with us. She does not get a bowl of food placed somewhere else in the room. We eat on the couch in the living room, and Amber eats with us on the couch. She likes her food placed on the couch, which can be messy. We always have a cup of water for her so she doesn't have to jump off the couch to go to her water bowl.

Some dog books say that you have to feed the dog last. That would not work with Amber, who is part of the family and eats at the same time if not a little sooner than we do. On a typical day, Amber eats one meal, but on weekends and on vacation, she gets two meals a day.

Amber can drink tap water, but we give her spring water. We have been told that it improves her coat and Amber has a beautiful coat. Amber especially likes ice in her water, so make sure you have lots of ice in the freezer.

Amber loves dog cookies and she understands that word. She especially loves peanut butter flavor cookies and, since she is a small dog, she particularly likes bite-sized little cookies. She communicates her desire for cookies frequently by going to the place in the house where cookies are kept, looking up and sometimes talking in a low little growl. Amber probably dreams about cookies, as she sometimes licks Daddy's ear in the middle of the night in an attempt to get cookies.

Because we are concerned about Amber's weight, we will give her cookies only after she finishes her dinner. This is a ritual—she expects the cookies after dinner. After a few cookies, you have to explain to her that she had enough cookies, and that she will have more cookies tomorrow. Amber will keep growling for more cookies, but she realizes that there is a limit to the number of cookies she can have and she will eventually stop growling.

We only buy dog treats manufactured in the United States or Canada, so please check the packages for the origin of the treats.

If you have food delivered, Amber will sometimes go crazy at the sight of the food delivery person. Amber will also bark if the telephone rings because she associates the telephone ringing with the concierge advising us that a food delivery is on its way.

As you know, Amber loves to eat at restaurants. More on that later.

Amber with a meal prepared for her at an outdoors restaurant.

Equipment

Amber has several pieces of equipment of which you must be aware.

Amber is walked with a harness rather than with a collar. Because Amber, as a Pomeranian, is susceptible to having a collapsing trachea, a harness is better for her breathing than a leash around her neck. It is hard to describe here how to put a harness on a dog, and there are several different types of harnesses. Your pet store or veterinarian will help you and it is easy once you get the hang of it. Make sure that the harness is not too loose or too tight, and that it is not twisted on her.

Amber has leashes that match her harnesses. They are six feet long rather than four feet long to give her maximum freedom while walking. There are several leashes that look like tape measures that extend further, but they are flimsy and we don't feel comfortable with them. Leashes should have medium hooks- not too heavy and not too lightweight.

For grooming between visits to the groomer, we have a comb and brush, a blow dryer, shampoo, and a nail grinder.

Amber sleeps in many different locations during the night, but she has a small pink bed with a built-up rim upon which she can rest her head. If that bed needs to be replaced, find a bed that has a rim rather than a purely flat bed. The bed has to be a medium size—Amber will not feel secure in a large bed. At times, Amber will sleep under a table that she thinks is her den. (Indeed, if you can't find Amber immediately, she is likely under a table). Amber likes to be covered with a thin blanket as it makes her feel secure, and Amber snoring is a sign that she is in the midst of a good sleep.

For the car, Amber has several soft mats, a dog-bone shaped pillow, and a soft blanket. Amber loves pillows and blankets, the softer the better. Towels and washcloths should be handy if it rains or if Amber walks in a puddle. We do not have a formal dog seat as Amber would not stay in it.

The most important equipment we have for Amber is her stroller. We saw one for the first time at a dog show (a wonderful place to obtain information), and we bought it from one of the many dog shops on the Internet. It was easy to assemble, and Amber likes being transported in it when she is tired. Amber even motions to us when she wants to go in the stroller.

The stroller, which folds up neatly in the trunk of the car, has storage below and cup holders for her water and Mommy's coffee. The stroller allows us to take Amber to dog-friendly stores and outdoor restaurants and concerts. You will hear oohs and ahs from many people who have never seen a dog in a stroller, and many dog owners will stop you and ask you where you bought it. We keep a soft mat at the bottom of the stroller seat to make Amber more comfortable and we make sure that her legs are OK if she is in the stroller for a long time. You must also tie Amber's leash to the stroller for added security.

Another important piece of equipment is her name tag. Make sure that her tags have the phone number of someone other than yourself who can take Amber in an emergency. Recently, a senior citizen neighbor fell while walking her dog and Daddy, seeing the neighbor, took the dog to safety while the neighbor was taken to the hospital. Daddy noticed that the dog tags only had the neighbor's phone number when it should have had the emergency cell number of someone who ordinarily does not walk the dog.

Amber has a water bowl in the shape of a large Cosmopolitan glass but not a food bowl. She has several toy boxes for her toys—she likes toy boxes that are low enough for her to reach and select toys independently.

For restaurants, we have a mat that Amber can eat off of. Sometimes, we use the mat to cover a chair Amber can sit on while eating.

You must keep on hand a supply of "flossies" (long curly pieces of beef bones) both at home and in the car. Amber likes dark and thick flossies, rather than light and skinny flossies, and prefers the jumbo to the regular size since they are longer and easier for her to hold with her paws. If Amber has chewed on a flossie for a long time to the point where it is short, take it away from her. We don't want her to choke on a flossie.

Keep on hand some wee-wee pads. If you place them in a particular area of the house, Amber will find them and use them at night and save you from having to walk her at 3 a.m.

While this is not technically equipment, if you leave Amber home for any length of time, make sure you leave the television and lights on. On a day on which both Mommy and Daddy work, Amber gets to watch Oprah before Mommy and Daddy.

Don't forget to have lots of disposable cameras around, both in the house and in the car. You never know when Amber is going to produce a "Kodak Moment."

Amber in her stroller.

Clothing

We don't know if Amber will need clothing if you remain in Florida, but this is written in the event you move to a location colder than Florida.

Amber has a large selection of jackets, sweaters, and rain gear. She has or has had a beaded dress, a denim jacket, a plaid Burberry coat, a pink checked jacket that looks like something Audrey Hepburn would have worn, several leather jackets, a suede jacket, a parka for cold weather, a windbreaker, several wooly sweaters, and a variety of vinyl raincoats. We generally do not buy her clothing other than for protection from the weather.

Amber's size is usually 16, and she looks best in pink, red or brown. She also looks best in more feminine looking clothing. She is better in outfits that are not difficult to put on—clothing with zippers and snaps are more difficult than clothing with Velcro and avoid outfits that require you to put all four of her legs into the outfit. Make sure Amber's clothing has a hole through which you can attach her leash to her harness—if not, have a tailor sew a hole in the appropriate place.

Amber loves to try on clothing. As you know, Amber won a "Dog of the Month" contest with a local television station. In a "dogumentary" video produced about her, she was filmed trying on clothing at Aunt Pat's dog clothing store in Southampton.

Amber has had some nice pieces of harness jewelry, but they seem to quickly fall off.

Our most important clothing purchase during the year is Amber's Halloween costume. We start the search for the perfect Halloween costume in July. Amber has been a witch, a bunny, a fairy princess, a party girl, and a court jester. She marches every year in a Halloween parade sponsored by her Aunt Pat and she has won for being "best witch" and "most whimsical."

Amber modeling.

Amber wearing her Burberry jacket on her third birthday.

Toys

Amber loves toys. She has two cellphones, an i-pod, a surfboard, a bottle of Dog Perignon champagne, many shoes and pocketbooks, and a zooful of giraffes, monkeys, bears, hippos, ducks and doggies. All of these, of course, are stuffed and plush and you would be amazed what toys they make for dogs. She even had a stuffed Hillary Clinton dog toy.

In buying toys for Amber, choose toys that are small enough to fit in her mouth but not so small that she could swallow them. None of Amber's toys have buttons or any small items that Amber could possibly pull apart and eat.

Amber likes to throw and fling toys. Therefore, you must buy toys that have lots of legs or arms, or things that Amber can sink her teeth into and throw. Amber also likes to put toys in her mouth and squeak them, so you must buy toys that have good squeakers that make loud noises. Don't be shy about testing noisemakers and testing toys on Amber in general.

Some dog toys have talking voices. Amber does not care for these toys, just as she does not like a local nursery that has talking Santas and snowmen at Christmas.

Amber seems to love ducks more than any other type of toy. The first toy she had was a soft yellow duck that Amber used to wrap herself around. When Amber was younger, she would wake Daddy in the middle of the night to play the game "Throw Duckie Off the Bed" where she would play with the duck, throw the duck off the bed, and then expect Daddy to retrieve the duck so Amber could do the same thing again.

Amber's favorite toy is Rowdy. Rowdy is a medium-sized stuffed Eskimo dog that Mommy won at a carnival shortly before Amber was born. When Amber was a baby, we often found her tucked between Rowdy's paws, possibly thinking that Rowdy was her mommy. When Amber grew larger, she would wrestle with Rowdy and occasionally hump him. Rowdy is in poor shape and smells pretty badly, but Amber would be devastated if we ever tried to get rid of him.

We donate Amber's old toys (and clothing) to a dog shelter. Amber is well aware of her possessions and gets very possessive, so you have to explain to her that she no longer needs the items and that she can help some poor dogs less fortunate than herself. Better yet, try to accumulate these items when she is sleeping.

Amber and her toys at the Plaza Hotel.

Communication

Amber is very intelligent and can communicate with you and understand what you are saying.

If Amber is hungry, she will stick her tongue out and go, as we say, "licky licky". She will point to her closed Starbucks water cup in the car if she wants water, and will engage in loud breathing if she wants the heat turned off or the air conditioner turned on or higher in the house or the car. If she wants a cookie, Amber will stand at the place where the cookies are located and growl in a low voice or stare or, in the middle of the night, lick your ears and face. Amber will sit at the front door or bark when she wants to go out.

Amber will roll over in the grass if she is happy and will turn over on her back on her bed if she is content. Amber will often turn over on her back to say that she wants a tummy rub—Amber loves tummy rubs and especially loves the area under her chin massaged.   If Amber wants you to play with her, Amber will bring a toy over to you to throw so that she can retrieve it and then bring it back to you.

She understands the words "Mommy", "Daddy", "Grandma", "Amber", "dog", "chicken" (generic word for all food), "cookies", "squirrel", "rabbit", "horsies", "duckies", "goats", "kite", "good girl" and "out."   She knows that she is Amber, and that dogs are like herself.   With regard to the words "dog", "squirrel", "rabbit" and "kite", we sometimes have to spell those words out so that she doesn't scream.

Try carrying out a conversation with Amber in English with complicated words that she doesn't know.   She will listen to you very intently, and then tilt her head as if to indicate that she thinks you are crazy.   Daddy tried to teach Amber about geography during the 2008 Presidential election (e.g., Amber is from Missouri and now lives in New York, Grandma and Uncle Craig live in Florida, Amber traveled across Indiana, Ohio and Pennsylvania when she was a baby), and Amber thought Daddy was nuts.

Amber gets very upset when she hears the words "Oh, no", so don't use them.   Amber knows the meaning of the word "no" and doesn't like it, so please use that word only when absolutely necessary.   Amber understands "good girl, no barkee", which we use if we don't want her to bark at another dog or a kite on the beach.   Amber likes to be praised, so use the phrase "good girl" frequently, especially when she urinates or defecates.

Never, never use the expression "Yappy Hour"—Amber knows what that is.   A now-defunct dog store held a party for dogs and their parents every Saturday afternoon called "Yappy Hour."   Unfortunately, a few male dogs at the parties attempted to sniff Amber's rear end and Amber did not appreciate that.   Amber associated "Yappy Hour" with those dogs and she did not want to go to "Yappy Hour."

While Amber understands "sit" and "stay", Amber has not been taught the usual pet tricks, such as "give me your paw." Some people will ask Amber for her paw, and she gives nothing in return.

In general, Amber does not like sudden movements or noises—she will bark loudly at squirrels, rabbits, kites, wind, umbrellas, signs and flags that move, helicopters, low-flying planes, motorcycles, street cleaners, snow plows, and sand rakers. Grandma, you may remember the time we went to the beach with you and the umbrella kept blowing over due to the wind and Amber not liking the umbrella. Also, Amber especially does not like "Mr. Vacuum" and tells him to go back to the closet.

Do not take Amber to fireworks on the Fourth of July—we have tried that a couple of times and Amber has warned us not to do it again. Just as Amber's nose is very sensitive, her ears are sensitive as well. She has also advised us that she does not like thunder, even though we tell her that it is Uncle Craig bowling and that if it is particularly loud, that Uncle Craig has just bowled a strike.

Playing

Amber loves to play.

Her favorite game is for you to throw toys down the hall or in the backyard so she can retrieve them and have you throw them again. She will do this two or three times before stopping. Amber also loves to fling toys by their arms or legs or tags, and she likes to make music with squeaky toys.

Amber likes to hide in pillows and her bed and comforter. She will rearrange her pillow, bed, or comforter so she is in the coziest spot possible.

Amber insists on making a game about going out. If you try to put the harness and leash on her, she will run around very excited but will not put herself in a position to allow you to put her equipment on. She is only ready to go out when she places herself close enough to allow you to put her harness and leash on.   Therefore, if you are going out with Amber, you must leave extra time for this ritual.

As we mentioned before, Amber loves to chase animals, especially squirrels and rabbits.   She has even chased a chipmunk, a rooster, and some guinea fowl. We don't know if this is a game or whether Amber is looking for food, and we really don't want to find out.

Amber hiding under her table.

Amber hanging with her stuffed friend.

Other Dogs

As best we can tell, Amber does not like other dogs.

The only dogs Amber has reacted well to are peaceful older dogs who are about her size. Large dogs frighten Amber, as do hyperactive smaller dogs. The two dogs she has liked most were an older Maltese named Brutus with whom she sometimes had high-pitched conversations and an older Pekingese in her building named Yo-Yo whom she occasionally kisses.

If Amber sees a dog coming down the street while we are walking her, she will often plop herself down where she is, smile, wait for the dog, scream at the dog when it passes, and then sniff the spots where the dog has urinated. Amber will sometimes follow dogs so she can scream at them and then smell the spots where they had urinated. We really aren't positive whether Amber hates these dogs or just has a strange way of communicating with them.

If we see a much larger dog coming towards us while walking Amber, we move her to the other side of the street. If it is a pit bull, we pick Amber up and move away as quickly as possible. Pit bulls have been known to kill small dogs like Pomeranians.

Amber sometimes engages in blood-curdling screams at other dogs, and Mommy sometimes calls Amber "Cujo" or "The Terrorist". Do not be frightened, as Amber means no harm. Again, we don't know if a scream means she hates the dog or whether she has a weird manner of communication with other dogs. However, never put Amber in an elevator with another dog—Amber does not share elevator space well.

We try to take Amber to as many dog events as possible so that she can attempt to socialize with other dogs. Sometimes, and especially when she is tired, she does not mind the other dogs. This is especially true if there are many other dogs and she feels overwhelmed. If she has too much energy, watch out.

Amber did have a bad experience at a dog park when she was younger—a dog jumped on her back and Daddy had to separate the two dogs. Since then, Amber much prefers dog-friendly people parks to dog parks and we don't take Amber to traditional dog parks.

Considering the variety of breeds of dogs, we are always amazed that Amber can distinguish between any dog regardless of breed and any other type of mammal.

People

What do Grandma, Aunt Pat, our maid Aunt Olga, Greg, a handsome young construction foreman who used to live in our building, Mario, a porter in our building, Luis, our middle-aged dry cleaner, and Omar, a senior citizen concierge, have in common? Nothing, except for the fact that Amber goes especially crazy over these people. She will run around in a crazy pattern and bark incessantly in a nice manner when she sees these people. Amber realizes that these people especially love her, and can sense which people especially love dogs.

Amber can also sense which people do not like dogs. We had a sour neighbor who did not like dogs (or people for that matter), and Amber avoided her. Amber will not waste her time on mean people, and Amber ignoring a person is the worst form of insult.

Amber is egalitarian. Amber goes crazy over our maid, but had no reaction to a number of famous people while she was on the set of a local television program. Amber is not a reverse snob; she just needs to see the right celebrity. She (and Daddy) were not too unhappy when beautiful Dylan Lauren (Ralph Lauren's daughter) pushed aside a bevy of people after her interview on the television show just to play with Amber.

Please keep in mind that since Amber can be overly enthusiastic with some people, you must use some discretion. While Amber has never bitten anyone, Amber is still an animal. While Amber enjoys human activities, she is not a little person in a fur coat. You don't need any lawsuits or, worse, Amber destroyed if she bites anyone.

Perhaps the hardest part of living with Amber, at least for Daddy, is dealing with mean people. Daddy is amazed at how many people have been nasty to Amber as well as how many people hate dogs. Daddy especially remembers a man running out of a multi-million dollar home, yelling at Daddy and Amber "Get da ******' dawg off da ******' lawn" when Amber was not even on the guy's lawn.

The policemen in our usually laid-back city have also been particularly nasty. Daddy and Amber have been stopped for walking in areas where there must have been invisible "no dog" signs posted. Another cop asked Daddy to show that he had two poop bags as that was supposedly a city law (it isn't). Dogs are not allowed on the beach or boardwalk in our city, even off-season, and a cop who said that Pomeranians were more vicious than pit bulls gave Daddy a ticket for walking Amber on the boardwalk on a rainy mid-week off-season day.

As much as Daddy has wanted to punch out some of his obnoxious neighbors, not to mention the obnoxious policemen, Daddy realizes that Amber does not like signs of anger or emotion. Say that you're sorry, and move on if you encounter anyone obnoxious. Amber does not like confrontations, and we don't have to tell you that there are a lot of crazy people out there. Instead, think of some alternatives. When Daddy got the ticket for walking Amber on the boardwalk, he called his friends in City Hall and told them that he would have the local law declared invalid by a court if the ticket were not dropped. The ticket was dropped. Also, if we had more time in our lives, we would start a campaign to make our dog-unfriendly city government adopt more dog-friendly policies.

With regard to children, Amber loves children and children love Amber. However, Mommy and Daddy are always astounded by how many children will come up to pet Amber without even asking Mommy and Daddy whether they can pet her.

Mommy and Daddy differ slightly on how Amber should be handled around children. Fearing possible lawsuits leading to judgments and/or euthanasia for Amber, Mommy's view is that no child should be allowed to pet Amber. Daddy believes that since Amber loves children, on rare occasions, he will allow children to touch Amber. However, the conditions are as follows: (a) if Amber is tired or hungry or does not want to be bothered, no children will be allowed to pet Amber; (b) no unsupervised child may pet Amber; and (c) only extremely well-behaved children in the company of a responsible adult will have a chance to pet Amber, and that is conditional upon Amber's reaction to the child. If Amber gets too wild, the visit is over.

In her seven years, Amber has met a variety of people from a variety of social, racial, ethnic, and economic backgrounds. She is comfortable with everyone, so long as they are nice to her.

Walking Miss Amber

Amber loves to walk, and there are rules to learn connected to her walking.

First and foremost, Amber never goes outside without a harness and leash. While Amber would probably not veer into the street, she could wander into a street to chase a loud vehicle or animal. A friend of ours just lost her Pomeranian who darted into a busy street to chase a motorcycle. Make sure that the harness is secure and that the leash is correctly fastened. Even then, harnesses and leashes can break, so please be very careful walking her.

We let Amber choose the direction of her walk. The direction in which Amber walks is based on her sense of smell. Amber starts her walk by putting her nose up to the air to see which direction has the most interesting dog smells. She wants to see what dogs have walked in her neighborhood, and Amber's sniffing and smelling where dogs have been previously is the equivalent of our reading a newspaper. A typical walk is 30-40 minutes, but sometimes Amber will walk for an hour. Rain seems to enhance dog smells, so her walks just after it rains tend to be longer. Also, if the weather is too miserable for a walk in the morning, Amber will want to walk longer later in the day.

In Florida, you may have to give her shorter walks and you will probably have to walk her in the early morning or late evening due to the heat.

Bring poop bags, as Amber uses her walks to defecate. If Amber is inspecting an area particularly intensely, it means that she is about ready to make a doody. Amber makes doody on average once a day. The color does not matter, and it changes daily with the food she eats. Make sure that the doody is not too soft. If Amber has diarrhea, give her rice from a Chinese restaurant as that hardens the doody just as it does for people.

We never allow Amber in the street, especially in the busy neighborhood we live in. A nearby building on an especially busy street has a sign saying "Curb Your Dog." We ignore it as we would never put Amber into the busy street. Amber's safety comes before any stupid signs.

An issue in our neighborhood is whether Amber can walk on the grassy area between the sidewalk and the street. Our policy is that if someone has planted shrubbery in and taken special care of their grassy area, we don't touch it. If someone has done nothing to their grassy area, it's fair game. Many of the grassy areas are doggy hot spots and Amber knows all of the doggy hot spots.

Amber likes to walk in a variety of neighborhoods. She likes to walk in cities and main streets in small towns and villages because she can smell many dogs on her route and stop into her favorite stores for cookies. Amber likes to walk in fields where she can roll around in goose dung or certain patches of grass that, to her, smell wonderful. Amber likes vacant lots, dog-friendly people parks, and, on some occasions, the beach. In our neighborhood, Amber has a definite preference for some blocks over others.

Amber is not a water dog. She does not like the ocean, and jumps over puddles in the street. While she likes snow, Amber will sometimes not walk in the rain, and does not like wind.

Besides dogs, squirrels and rabbits, she screams at motorcycles, street cleaners, and loud vehicles. In those circumstances, you must have full control over her.

Amber will tell you when she wants to go out and when she wants to come in. Make sure that you have water ready for her at the end of her walk, as well as a towel to dry her off on a rainy day.

Amber will stop during a walk and watch activity, such as birds (she loves birds), gardeners or boys playing basketball. She will make herself at home by plopping down on the sidewalk and stretching herself out. However, Amber does not like construction sites. A building near us was recently constructed using a huge crane and Amber would insist on walking on the other side of the street rather than in front of the crane.

Lime and other chemicals placed on grass, standing water filled with gasoline or antifreeze and salt placed on sidewalks are all bad for Amber—keep her way from these conditions as well as puddles in general. Watch out for chicken bones, dead birds, and nuts that have sticky thorns. Something with sticky thorns once attached itself to Amber's vagina and it was no fun removing it. Make sure that Amber is in the shade as often as possible and makes sure that she does not walk on hot asphalt or sidewalks.

Of course, please let no big dogs near Amber, and especially pit bulls. We even watch to see if the dogs walked near Amber are under the control of their owner and we don't let Amber near any dog that does not appear to be under control.

We do not allow Amber to walk across a busy street herself; we pick her up and cross her. We are also astounded by all of the idiots who are on their cell phones at the same time as they are walking their dog. Because of all of the possible distractions, walking Amber will require your full attention.

Besides being great exercise, walking Amber in our neighborhood gives us a chance to meet the people in the neighborhood and see what is going on. Of course, Amber is interested in everything.

Driving Miss Amber

Amber loves to ride in the car. However, she does have her limits. Two consecutive hours is about all she can handle. Otherwise, she starts to yawn and appears stressed.

If she is driving with Daddy alone, she will sit on her mat in the front passenger seat. It is not the safest place for her as the air bag, if inflated, could crush her. Nonetheless, Amber thinks that Daddy needs a co-pilot and Amber is right.

If Mommy is driving with Daddy, Amber will go the back seat and either sleep on her dog bone pillow or cuddle next to Mommy (who sits in the back seat) and rest. She is especially cute when she is snuggled next to Mommy, and Daddy would like an Ambercam so he can watch Amber as he is driving. Amber also likes to put her nose up to the air vents in the middle of the back seat so she can take full advantage of the air conditioning. She will breathe heavy if she wants the heat turned off or the air conditioning turned on or up higher.

If Amber is not sleeping, we will tell Amber if there are sights outside of the window (dogs, squirrels, rabbits, kites and horses) that she might be interested in. Sometimes, we roll down the window so that Amber can bark at the dogs outside.

Amber loves drive-up food stands like McDonald's, Burger King and Starbucks. She likes when the people at the window pay attention to her, and some of them will reward her with a treat. The TD Bank drive-up (we understand that they are in Florida) is one of her favorites as it always has a tray of dog treats ready for dog visitors. Amber will remind the teller that she is a dog and thus entitled to a dog treat.

Amber does not like sudden movement. Therefore, try to drive slower and make turns and curves more gently in the car with Amber. Remember that when you drive with Amber, you are driving with precious cargo.

If you have driven more than an hour, try to stop and take Amber out to pee-pee. Of course, never ever leave Amber in the car alone. You won't have to worry about that as Amber would scream at you if you attempted to do that. Even if Daddy and Mommy are driving together and Daddy has to make a stop, Amber will usually scream at Daddy and insist that Daddy take her with him.

Amber likes ice water in the car, so always make sure that you have some available. Make sure that your trunk is equipped with the stroller, mats for the stroller, cameras, towels, blankets, and some bowls in case you are going to a restaurant with Amber.

As Amber also likes shade, the car must be parked in a shady spot. If there is no shade, try to keep the windows down so that it is not too hot for Amber when she returns to the car. Please remember to put the air conditioning on full blast once you return Amber to the car.

Just a reminder that Amber does not like outbursts of emotion. Therefore, please do your best to refrain from road rage. We understand that will be tough in Florida.

Finally, when you ride with Amber, make sure that the leash is off and that there are never any doors open from which she could escape This may sound silly, but dogs have choked where their leashes were caught in car doors and have escaped through open doors. Also, make sure her harness and any clothing are off as Amber likes to ride in the nude.

Amber modeling while driving.

Places Amber Likes to Visit

Just about everywhere but the veterinarian. Indeed, when Amber goes into New York City where her vet is located, she is always a little apprehensive that she is going to be taken there.

Amber likes sidewalks in towns and cities that have many dogs, outdoor restaurants, hotels, stores, outdoor concerts, fields, dog-friendly people parks that are well-maintained, vacant lots and the beach (sometimes). She will be glad to visit any dog-friendly store and besides dog-related stores, particularly likes to go to the dry cleaner, the bank, the photo shop where all of her pictures are developed, the barber shop, the one dog-friendly post office in our area, and our local convenience store where they know her by name. She loves stores that have dog biscuits waiting for their dog customers, and is usually pretty good in determining which stores have dog treats behind the counter.

Besides dog events which will be discussed later, Amber likes to visit places that have animals. Like any little girl, she loves horses. She loves going to watch polo so she can tell the horses when they are out of bounds and she can sniff what the horses have left behind during half-time. She goes to a horse show once a year and plops herself down at a particular shaded location so she can watch the horses run around a ring. We also go to an outdoor restaurant where Amber likes to see the goats, and a winery where Amber loves to visit the tortoises and alpacas. While the animals usually ignore Mommy and Daddy, they stand up and greet Amber as if she were some type of celebrity.

Amber loves crafts fairs, and especially the ones where they sell kettle corn and people leave kettle corn droppings for her to pick up. If you take her to a crafts fair that allows dogs, make sure you go early before it gets too sunny and crowded and make sure that she always has shade and water. Some "no dog" fairs will allow her if she is kept in the stroller, just as other places that say "no dogs" are not always that black and white when they see the stroller.

Because of the possibility of ticks, we keep Amber out of wooded areas. Areas where there are too many people are also off limits for Amber as she needs her space. Of course, no fireworks.

Amber has done a lot of wonderful things you wouldn't normally think are for dogs. She has ridden in a horse and carriage in Central Park, has walked around the perimeter of Shea Stadium, and has been interviewed (really) on a television program. Amber has stayed at the Plaza Hotel in New York City (twice) and ate outdoor brunch at Tavern on the Green. She had afternoon tea in a fancy hotel in Philadelphia and celebrated her seventh birthday inside of a French bistro in the Hamptons.

Amber watching the horses at the Hamptons Classic.

Store Etiquette

Amber loves to visit stores, but we have various protocols regarding store visits.

First, we only take Amber to stores that we know are or believe to be dog-friendly. We will not bring Amber into stores that are too congested or sell food. We generally use the stroller for Amber in stores.

As Amber can get excited around strangers, we make sure that people play with her only for a limited amount of time.   Store clerks like to play with Amber, but we have to limit Amber's playing with the clerks so she does not disturb the other customers.   While Amber generally knows how to behave in a store and usually acts like a lady, we always remember that we are guests in the store and that we could be disinvited as well.

This may sound cruel, but if you find a store that allows Amber to visit, keep it to yourself.   If there are too many dogs in the store, or if a dog unfriendly person gets wind of the store's policy and goes to the Board of Health, Amber may not be invited back to visit.   We appreciate the books and websites that tell you what places are dog-friendly, but we are always concerned that they could end up making places dog unfriendly.

Make sure that Amber always has water in the store.   If the store is too hot or has other dogs that Amber does not like, take Amber out immediately.   Amber will motion to the exit when she has had enough of a store, so take her out when she tells you that she wants to leave.

Restaurants

We have had some wonderful outdoor dining experiences with Amber.   More than one restaurant knows Amber by name, and some even know her favorite meals.   At a restaurant in the Hamptons, it is wood-grilled chicken with penne or rigatoni dipped in olive oil.   At a restaurant nearer to us, we try to visit on "roasted chicken" night as Amber particularly loves the roasted chicken at that restaurant.

In choosing restaurants for Amber, we look for places that are not congested and will have both proteins and carbs for her to eat.   Restaurants that have tables stacked up against each other or restaurants that only serve French fries as vegetables usually do not work.

Some outdoor restaurants only allow you to have dogs at certain tables or in certain positions—one outdoor restaurant built on a platform insisted that we had to have Amber sit off the platform in "bungee dog" style. We left that restaurant since that was unacceptable to us and we still call that the "bungee dog" restaurant even though it mercifully closed several years ago.

Although people love to see Amber in the stroller, placing Amber in a stroller at a restaurant is not our first choice. Amber does not always like to eat in the stroller in warm weather. Rather, we look for restaurants with enough room so we can place her on her mat and feed her from there. If the restaurant is empty, we will even put her on a mat on a chair. Restaurants with low chairs and low tables work better than restaurants with high chairs and high tables.

We do not go to restaurants which are too close to the street or have too many distracting children. We love restaurants surrounded by lots of open space—there are several of those in the Hamptons and Amber especially loves those restaurants.

Some tips for ordering. Always ask first for lots of napkins and ice or ice water for Amber. As you know, Amber loves ice water. Always order for yourself a back-up that Amber can eat in the event Amber does not like the meal you thought she would like. Turn down the bread—we don't want Amber staring at the bread. Also, no French fries—Amber can sniff French fries a mile away. We always bring our own plates and cups, as we don't want Amber eating off of restaurant plates, cups or silverware.

Since Amber is a small dog, her food must be chopped into little pieces and cannot be too hot. With regard to vegetables at a restaurant, pasta and potatoes are easier to serve Amber than smaller vegetables like peas and rice. Always ask if the restaurant has shredded carrots as Amber loves shredded carrots. Also, presentation means something to Amber, so try to serve her foods that have some sizzle. One of Amber's favorites is chicken and steak fajitas (without onions), both from the smell and the sizzling sound.

Always order Amber's food with "no onions" and "no cheese and "no sauce". You'd be surprised how many restaurants will throw onions, cheese and sauce into meals you would never expect to contain onions, cheese and sauce. We're amazed by this, particularly because people could be allergic to onions, cheese, and sauce. As onions (like chocolate) can be deadly to Amber, you also have to be careful that onions have not been chopped into hamburgers or other food or used as a marinade for brisket or other meats. Therefore, you must ask restaurants about their use of onions, onion powder, or scallions in any form. We go as far as to taste test certain foods we suspect may have or be seasoned with onions before serving them to Amber.

You will meet many lovely waiters and waitresses and restaurant owners as well as other dog-friendly guests who will come over to visit Amber. However, remember that you want to be invited back to the restaurant, and that Amber can get overly friendly at times. Also, we do extensive work cleaning up the floor, so no one can accuse Amber of being a pig. Most people say that Amber is better behaved in restaurants than children, and she is.

Again, if you learn of a good dog-friendly restaurant, don't spill the beans. If there are too many dogs the next time you show up, Amber may not be welcomed.

Just as she is with people, Amber is not a food snob. She has eaten at many fancy restaurants (and Grandma, you may remember the French restaurant that let her eat inside), but she likes grilled chicken at the McDonald's and Burger King drive-ups as well. Indeed, if Amber does not like the meal you serve her, Burger King grilled chicken almost always works.

Amber inside of a restaurant for her seventh birthday.

Hotels

Amber behaves well in hotels, with a few small tips.

Hotels come in three categories. The best category is hotels that are totally dog friendly. Those are like the hotel in Philadelphia that had seven varieties of dog treats at the front desk, concierges that remembered Amber's name, long hallways to run down, and room service. Also in that category is a hotel in the Hamptons as well as one in our hometown that have "doggie menus."

The next category is "dog tolerant hotels", those that allow dogs in only a few select rooms and restrict dogs from some public places. Those are not our first choice, but will do if there are no dog friendly hotels available. Finally, there are the "no dogs" hotels which we of course avoid. There are several websites that list dog friendly hotels, but call the hotel in advance to make sure that the hotel policies haven't changed. Some hotels have fees for dogs and some only permit small dogs like Amber.

The best hotels for Amber are those with large grounds or are near parks like Central Park. Rooms with fenced-in patios are especially good for Amber, as she can stay outside in a protected area.

With regard to high-rise hotels, pick a room that is in a quiet area not near the elevator, possibly one that is at the end of the corridor. In a low-rise hotel, a room on the first floor near the outside door is preferable in the event Amber needs to use the facilities.

Amber loves room service. Most room service menus have dog-friendly items like hamburgers and turkey club sandwiches. Amber eats on the bed with Mommy and Daddy, and will sleep there as well. Nice hotels have many pillows, and Amber snuggles up in all of them.

Try to find rooms that are not adjacent to rooms with other dogs, as Amber can carry on a conversation with a neighboring dog in the middle of the night. Generally, though, Amber will sleep through the night and is a good hotel guest.

If you are packing to go to a hotel, you have to pack Amber's items at the same time as you pack your own. You can never give Amber the impression that she is going to be left behind. For Amber, you need to pack her brush and comb, some clothing, some toys, and a few flossies. You do not need to pack Amber's bed as she will sleep on the bed with you. When you are packing to leave a hotel, pack Amber's belongings last so she does not get upset.

Finally, make sure that you are aware of a 24/7 emergency vet in the area where you will be traveling with Amber.

Amber at the Rittenhouse Hotel in Philadelphia.

Celebrating New Year's Eve at the Garden City Hotel, Garden City, New York.

Events

Through various sources, including our groomer, our veterinarian, the local newspaper, and some dog magazines, we learn of dog-related events.

We do dog walks for a lot of different charities. Daddy has a nice collection of tee-shirts from these events, and some of the events provide goody bags with many interesting dog items such as food, treats, toys and magazines.

As there are many dogs at these events, Amber is somewhat subdued and doesn't scream at the other dogs. The people attending these events are among the nicest people we have met—dog ownership does something positive to people.

There are four big events a year in Amber's life—her birthday, Halloween, Christmas/Chanukah and Valentines Day.

Amber's birthday is October 13th. For four of her first six birthdays, we took her to one of her favorite hotels in the Hamptons where all of the staff knew her by name and she would explore the hotel's five acres. This past year, a more upscale hotel in the Hamptons changed from "no dog" to "dog friendly" status and she had a wonderful time there. For her seventh birthday, we had a dog party in a shop that specializes in dog sorbet.

Amber's birthdays are always marked by a silly birthday hat saying "birthday princess" or something like that, a button saying "today I am....", a cake usually made by a local bakery specializing in dog bone cakes, a birthday bear or dog that sings "Happy Birthday," greeting cards, and toys. We sing to her "Happy Birthday" and play "Happy Birthday" on her music box for weeks before the special day. Amber does realize that her birthday is a special day, even if she does not understand why it is special.

For Halloween, Amber has a costume for Aunt Pat's parade and any other parades we learn about. The costume should be colorful, comfortable, and not too warm for Amber. To Amber's dismay, the costume usually involves a silly hat.

For Christmas/Chanukah, Amber has both a Christmas stocking and a Chanukah stocking which are filled with flossies and small dog toys. The stockings are placed over our fireplace, and Amber can tell when we put the flossies in as she jumps up and down for them when she catches their distinctive beefy scent. If she barks for a flossie, give it to her even if it is not yet Christmas or Chanukah and just purchase more for the holidays.

We have a Christmas tree with dog ornaments, many of which have Amber's picture. Amber has taken pictures with a variety of Santas and she likes Christmas light displays. At this time of year, Daddy performs for her a mini version of the Radio City Christmas Show (dancing bears, toy soldiers falling down).

Also at Christmas, we order our next year's calendar at Kinko's where Amber is the calendar girl for every month. We also order a photo album from an on-line company named Phoebe and Harry that will make a silk-screen cover out of the best Amber picture for the year.

Amber also receives presents for Valentines Day, and she helps us with the decorations around the house for that holiday.

Amber on her second birthday.

Amber as a fairy at Halloween.

End of Life

We hope that you think of the following: (a) how to handle Amber when she is near the end of her life and (b) what if your lives should end before Amber's.

We hope that unless Amber is suffering that badly and there is no hope for her recovery, you let Amber pass away in her sleep.

We also hope that you have a Plan B in the event you should happen to pass away before Amber.

In Conclusion

We know this is lengthy. However, Amber is worth every word of this guide. She is the most precious thing in our lives. If we do leave before Amber, please take good care of her and enjoy her and make sure that Amber remains as love-able and loving as she is right now.

Love,
Charlene and Bob